BASKETBALL

A GOLDEN SPORTS BOOK

by Ross Olney

illustrated by Ron Kjos

cover by Ben Otero

GOLDEN PRESS
Western Publishing Company, Inc.
Racine, Wisconsin

0-307-05602-3

CONTENTS

Our thanks to the following individuals and organizations
for their contributions to this book:

Cyndie, Mitch, and Jerry Speen
Joan Nemmert, The Los Angeles Forum
Mark Mano
The National Basketball Association
The Naismith Memorial Hall of Fame

CHAPTER 1

BASKETBALL GROWS UP

Basketball is truly an all-American game. It was invented in America (by a transplanted Canadian), it was first played in America, and it has become one of the most popular of all the American sports. Now the game is played throughout the world, but it all began, in its modern form, in an American gymnasium—as a replacement for boring physical exercises.

Basketball is a game in which the final score is very often not decided until the last seconds of regulation play—and quite often not even then. Since a basketball game cannot end in a tie, overtime periods are not at all unusual. Games often go into multiple overtime periods before a winner can be decided.

A game between Siena College and Niagara University, on February 21, 1953, lasted for *six* overtime periods before Niagara finally won.

Of course, the game can also go another way: A team called Bestwood once beat the Meadow Jets by a score of 242–20 in regulation time. This was probably not the most exciting game the fans saw that year!

It's a fact that soccer is the most widely *watched* sport in the world, but basketball is the most widely *played*. On trips through most residential areas in the United States, you won't see any soccer fields . . . but you will see dozens of backboards and hoops.

Basketball is a game of intense pressure. You can read the pressure on the players' faces and hear it in the screaming of the fans as the game progresses.

One incredible example of player pressure occurred during the East/West all-star game at Madison Square Garden in 1954. On the East team were superstars like Bob Cousy, Bill Sharman (now coach of the Los Angeles Lakers), Neil Johnston, and Harry "The Horse" Gallatin. On the West squad was the magnificent George Mikan, along with Jim Pollard, Bob Davies, Mel Hutchins, and Arnie Risen.

With just thirty-five seconds of regulation play left, East was leading 82–80. They had possession of the ball. This was before the advent of the 24-second clock and the rule that a team must shoot within this time period or lose the ball. So all the East team had to do to win the game was to stall until time ran out. Cousy, the brilliant Celtic, was a ball-control specialist. The seconds ticked away; the crowd was cheering for the great star from Boston. Suddenly Bob Davies streaked in, stole the ball, and drove downcourt, making an easy lay-up.

Now the score was 82–82. But the game wasn't over yet. East brought the ball upcourt quickly, Sharman fired and missed, Gallatin rebounded and passed to "Cooz." The Celtic ace aimed and shot; the ball swished through the net. With six seconds left, it was East over West, 84–82. The crowd was roaring.

George Mikan was unruffled. He knew that he would be set up for one last shot when West brought in the ball. Mikan's legendary skill under the basket was the main reason that the foul lane had been widened to 12 feet in pro

basketball, and it was he who kept the Lakers at the top of the standings. When the ball was passed in, West called for a time-out for a strategy meeting. Three seconds remained.

With time in, Pollard passed the ball to guard Bob Davies, and Davies whipped it to Mikan. Mikan turned quickly; his arm arced through the air just as the buzzer sounded. But the ball went far to the right of the basket.

Baltimore rookie of the year Ray Felix had struck Mikan's arm as he shot, fouling him. Pandemonium reigned at the Garden. The rafters shook with thunder from the packed stands. On the court, Mikan knew that the next action would be his—and his *alone*.

Since no time remained, the game was over. But since Mikan had been fouled, he would be allowed two shots. Police cleared the court of fans and players, and, all alone, Mikan stepped up to the foul line. The referee shook his head as he handed the ball to big George. If Mikan was ever going to break under pressure, the time had come.

With the floor literally shaking from the roaring of the fans, Mikan looked at the referee,

then at the ball, then at the basket. Carefully he bounced the ball twice; then, with one smooth, graceful motion, he flipped it toward the basket. It went through the hoop without touching. East 84, West 83.

Mikan smiled and accepted the ball from the referee for his second shot. He seemed not to hear the ear-battering noise from the East fans as they tried their best to unnerve him. Calmly he bounced the ball again, then tossed it. The noise died as the ball arched toward the basket.

Swish! The game went into overtime. One of the longest standing ovations ever heard at Madison Square Garden thundered down over Mikan. Even the most partisan of the East fans were now cheering for him. They knew he had endured tremendous pressure.

Ironically, it was Bob Cousy who was later voted the most valuable player of the game by sportswriters. In the overtime period that followed Mikan's two shots, "Cooz" scored 10 points, winning the game almost single-handedly for the East.

BUMPS AND BRUISES

Basketball demands an athlete with more physical skill and stamina than perhaps any other sport. He must be able to run, jump, pass, and take hard knocks, without any protective gear. He must be able to dribble with control and shoot with accuracy. And, importantly, he must be able to play both offense and defense, since basketball has no specialty squads.

Basketball was intended to be a "non-contact" sport, but in the midst of fast and furious action, players are bound to collide. Bumps and bruises, minor cuts, pulls and sprains, and, occasionally, broken bones are occupational hazards of the professional basketball player. Jerry West, formerly of the Los Angeles Lakers, has had his nose broken *eight times*. It's rumored that he had a provision in his contract to cover the cost of plastic surgery to his nose after his retirement.

THE BIG NOISE

Next to soccer fans, basketball fans are probably the most ardent and vocal in the world of sports. Their voices are usually contained in a closed room, so they sound even louder. Once, during a game between the Chicago Bulls and the Los Angeles Lakers, two players clashed. They were Bob Weiss, at that time of the Bulls, and Gail Goodrich of the Lakers. The Bulls are known in the National Basketball Association for rough play and great dramatic efforts to convince officials that they have been fouled.

The 1973 game was being played at the Forum in Los Angeles, home court of the Lakers. Weiss and Goodrich bumped, Weiss bumped back, Goodrich bumped back again, and then Weiss coiled up and took a swing at the popular Los Angeles guard. The crowded stands erupted in a thunder of boos and catcalls.

From that moment on, it was as if the noisy fans were being turned on and off by an electric switch. Each time Weiss got the ball, the ear-splitting noise from the spectators began. As soon as the ball left Weiss's hands, the noise instantly stopped.

It was a surprising and amusing example of 17,000 spectators being drawn together and voicing their team support as if on cue. The moral support offered by the noisy fans undoubtedly helped the players. Los Angeles won the game.

COMEBACK CHAMPIONS

Basketball is filled with astounding comeback efforts. Teams appearing to be hopelessly behind often manage to win in the last few seconds or after forcing the game into overtime periods.

Once a team came from behind to win in a very unusual way. In college basketball, there are two major tournaments to decide the top teams each year. In the National Invitational Tournament, the best teams in the country are invited to compete against each other. In the National Collegiate Athletic Association play-offs, the champions from each individual N.C.A.A. region compete.

In 1944, the University of Utah basketball team headed, with high hopes, for the N.I.T. games at Madison Square Garden. They were good and they knew it. But they were badly beaten in the very first round of the tournament. They started back home, weighted with disappointment.

On the way home, Utah was asked to stop over in Kansas to play in the Western finals of

the N.C.A.A. Tournament. Arkansas University had lost some players in an accident and could not compete. The Utah team had little to lose and everything to gain.

With the recent defeat still strong in their minds, they played an inspired game and won the Western finals. Then they went back to New York to play—and beat!—Dartmouth, the Eastern N.C.A.A. champions. Utah became the National N.C.A.A. champions.

In a strange twist of fate, they were then matched against St. John's University—the team that had won the N.I.T. play-offs from which Utah had originally been eliminated.

You guessed right: Utah won again. They went home, without further delay, as the undisputed kings of college basketball!

THE 'TROTTERS

There's no doubt that black players have made a more significant contribution to basketball than to any other team sport. To men like Wilt "The Stilt" Chamberlain, Kareem Abdul-Jabbar, Oscar Robertson, Walt Frazier, Elgin Baylor, Willis Reed, Bill Russell, and other black superstars, basketball is more a way of life than an entertaining game.

There is, however, a group of black players that looks at the game somewhat differently. Formed in 1927 by a white player named Abe Saperstein, the team has become world famous for playing its own special brand of basketball for fun and entertainment. The team is, of course, the Harlem Globetrotters.

At first the Globetrotters worked their way around the country, challenging local teams and accepting whatever pay they could get. They slept in their ancient bus, or in a convenient field, or even in a local jail when there was some extra room.

Soon they were beating everybody at serious basketball, and they began to clown their way through games.

Though spectators enjoyed the antics of the all-black Globetrotters team, few people actually took them seriously. In Canada, a local sportswriter said, "Any team could beat them in a real game."

The 'Trotters took that as a personal challenge. They met with, and beat, the Canadian all-star team 122–20! Many of the Canadians' 20 points resulted from stunts the 'Trotters just couldn't resist, even though they had decided to play serious basketball. They became more and more popular, playing games around the world for the entertainment of servicemen, royalty, and leaders of Iron Curtain countries.

Still, how could they hope to beat a real pro ball club, a club like the 1947–48 Minneapolis Lakers, for example? The Lakers boasted the great George Mikan, who was 6 feet 10 inches tall, and other basketball superstars. They were always at the top of the standings of the Basketball Association of America, predecessor of today's National Basketball Association.

The challenge was offered and accepted, and in February, 1948, a game was scheduled for Chicago Stadium. Though "Goose" Tatum, the 'Trotters center, was only 6 feet 3, his arms were long and his hands dangled down around his knees. A tight battle for rebounds was sure to develop between Goose and George Mikan, the rebound champion of the pros.

The game was not meant to be amusing; actually, it was a hard-fought battle to the finish for the so-called pro championship. By halftime, Minneapolis was leading 32–23, and

things looked bleak for the tired Harlem Globetrotters. Perhaps that Canadian sportswriter had been right, after all. What were they doing on the same court with the great Lakers? They felt foolish in the locker room as they tried to come up with some type of strategy that would stop the surging Minneapolis team. The 'Trotters were tired, but they weren't ready to quit.

As the second half started, the all-black team gambled and put three men on Mikan. This strategy began to work, and as the Lakers started to fade, the flashy ball-handling skills of the 'Trotters came into play. With one quarter left to play, the score was tied, 42–42.

With one minute left to play in the game, the score was again tied, 59–59, and the fans were shouting encouragement to both teams. In the final seconds, Elmer Robinson made a basket, and the Globetrotters won 61–59. The matter should have ended there, but it did not.

The Minneapolis Lakers were angry and embarrassed to have been beaten by a team of basketball clowns who generally took great pleasure in bending every rule in the book to complete their foolish stunts. A rematch was demanded and agreed upon.

One year later, again in Chicago, the 'Trotters met the B.A.A. champion Lakers, and once again, the 'Trotters were losing and discouraged at halftime. But then came their second-half second wind, and they began to hit the basket. When the third quarter ended, the 'Trotters were ahead 41–32 . . . and the fun began. The Globetrotters humiliated the Lakers in the final quarter, pulling out all the stops with between-the-legs passes, ball stealing and hiding, and remarkable "circus" shots the crowd couldn't believe. Meanwhile, they laughed and joked, totally demoralizing the Lakers, who knew they had lost the fight. The final score of 49–45 was rather tight, since the clowning of the 'Trotters allowed the Lakers to draw close again. However, they—and the basketball world—knew once and for all which team was really the best of all.

Though the Globetrotters are still an excellent basketball team, with several fine players, it is true that this probably could not happen against the superstars of today's pro basketball world.

Still, nobody has pushed for another match.

BASKETBALL FEBRUARY

HARLEM
GLOBETROTTERS
VS
MINNEAPOLIS
LAKERS

CHICAGO STADIUM

CHAPTER 2

A BASKETBALL QUIZ

Basketball is a relatively simple game to understand, though there are interpretations of the rules that make for interesting situations. The average basketball fan should do fairly well on the following quiz.

If you're just learning about basketball, the quiz will help you become familiar with some of the rules and judgment calls. Answers are on page 12.

1. In a hard-fought game between the Washington Bullets and the Atlanta Hawks, there's a battle going on for a rebound. Atlanta's Mike Sojourner tips the ball past the hoop; Lou Hudson tips it right back. Just as the ball passes above the basket, Elvin Hayes, of the Bullets, bats it away. Instantly the whistle blows.

What's the call?

2. The rules say that the ball cannot be kicked. While dribbling the ball downcourt, Keith Wilkes, of the Golden State Warriors, accidentally bounces the ball off his leg—directly into the hands of a teammate, who scores.

Does the score count?

3. In the days of the great George Mikan, some players wore eyeglasses, held in place with an elastic strap. Modern players generally wear contact lenses if they need vision correction. Abdul-Aziz, of the Houston Rockets, is trying to defend against a field goal attempt when his vision is suddenly blurred—he has lost one of his contact lenses.

Will an official stop the play until the lens can be found?

4. Cazzie Russell, of the Los Angeles Lakers, is fouled in the act of shooting. The foul causes an injury serious enough to take Russell out of the game, at least temporarily.

What about the free throw he has coming?

9

5. Walt Frazier is shooting three-to-make-two near the end of a game. Just as the ball leaves his hands for his final free throw, several of the opposing team members scramble into the free throw lanes, to be ready for any rebound. Frazier just stands there at the line.

Has a violation occurred?

6. The action has been so fast and furious between the Trailblazers of Portland and the Seattle Supersonics that 'Blazer Geoff Petrie finally fouls out. But the official scorer fails to notify the referee, and play continues with Petrie on the floor. Portland scores two quick field goals, one by Petrie himself, before the scorer's mistake is caught and the referee notified to remove Petrie from the game.

Does either of the field goals count?

7. In a game that has seesawed back and forth and been tied several times, the home team has possession. Coming downcourt, they know they need the field goal desperately. The ball handler flips the ball to a teammate, who quickly bounce passes to another teammate. But the pass hits the referee in the shoulder. Instantly, an opposing player grabs the ball and goes all the way for a lay-up.

Does the score count?

8. During a game between the Boston Celtics and the Buffalo Braves, one of the floor officials pulls a leg muscle and will not be able to continue officiating.

What happens?

9. This really happened in a pro game. During a successful field goal attempt by his own team, a ball boy (the helper who mops sweat from the floor under the basket and watches over team equipment) allowed a spare ball to roll out onto the floor. Instantly, the scored-upon team protested, claiming that the extra ball rolling and being kicked around confused them, allowing the score to be made.

What was the ruling?

10. This also really happened. Gail Goodrich, of the Lakers, was at the foul line to shoot two, but the Lakers were behind by 3 points and the time was almost gone. There seemed no chance to tie the score. Goodrich made the first shot easily, then purposely missed the second. The ball rebounded from the backboard and was instantly tipped in by a Laker teammate.

Did the Lakers get two points for the tip-in and tie the score?

11. In an unusually rough, physical game, a team finds itself in serious trouble in the fourth quarter: One by one, all of the starters have fouled out and have been replaced. Now, one of the last five players on the team fouls out—and there's nobody left on the bench to replace him.

What happens?

12. As two players from opposing teams scramble for possession of a loose ball the ball bounces out-of-bounds. Neither official saw exactly which player touched the ball last.

What will the referee do?

13. Austin Carr, of the Cleveland Cavaliers, is handed the ball for the first of two shots from the foul line. His attention is distracted by a scuffle in the stands, so he doesn't get the shot off right away. Suddenly the referee blows his whistle and takes the ball from Carr.

What happens now?

14. In the N.B.A. a team must shoot for a basket within twenty-four seconds after they gain possession; in the A.B.A., it's thirty seconds.

But when a player throws the ball in the direction of the basket, how do the officials know whether it's a shot or simply a pass?

ANSWERS

1. Goaltending, against Hayes. Extending directly upward from the rim of the basket is an imaginary cylinder. Whenever the ball is within this cylinder, no player can touch it (*except* for a player in the process of making a "dunk" shot). Goaltending will be called against any player who touches the ball within the cylinder—even if the ball is going *past* the hoop instead of *into* it.

2. Yes. Since the "kick" was really accidental, the officials will allow the play to stand. *Intentional* kicking of the ball is not allowed, but an accidental kick will not necessarily stop play.

3. No. The play will continue until one of Aziz's teammates gets the ball and calls for a time-out or until the ball is blown dead for some other reason. What if somebody steps on the lens in the meantime? *Crunch!* Too bad.

4. The opposing coach must select a replacement for Russell from the Lakers' bench to shoot the foul shots. As for Cazzie Russell, he can take a shower—he's through for the night. The rules say that any player who leaves a game because of an injury cannot return to that game, *unless* the injury was flagrant and intentional, like a punch in the jaw from an opponent.

5. No. In the pros, the rule on free throws says that the shooter cannot move from his position at the line until his shot strikes the backboard or the rim. The players lined up on the free throw lanes can move at the instant the ball leaves the shooter's hands. (In high school and college basketball, *nobody* can move until the free throw attempt strikes the backboard or rim.)

6. Yes. Both field goals count. Petrie will be removed from the game the moment the scorer informs the referee of his foul situation. Until then, points scored count.

7. Yes. The officials are considered a part of the floor. If a ball strikes one of them, it's still in play; it becomes a loose ball, up for grabs.

8. It depends on whether this is a regular season game or a play-off. During the regular season, the game would be continued minus one official. In all play-off games, however, there's a mandatory spare official waiting on the sidelines to fill in if one of the regular officials is unable to function.

9. The score was allowed to stand. Officials on the floor have the "power of elasticity" to make judgment calls when no specific rule covers a situation. In this case, it was the opinion of the officials that the spare ball did not interfere with the play.

10. No. The strategy was good, but Goodrich just hit the wrong spot. According to the rules, if the missed foul shot had bounced from the *rim* instead of the backboard, the score would have counted. The game would have been tied and gone into overtime.

11. The rules say that no team can be reduced to less than five players. The last player who was disqualified by fouls will remain in the game, and all additional fouls he commits will count as technical fouls *and* personal fouls.

12. He'll call for a jump ball between the two players at the nearest circle. This is the case whenever possession of the ball is uncertain and neither floor official can say who touched the ball last.

13. One of the rules on free throws is that the shot must be attempted within ten seconds after the ball is handed to the shooter by the referee. If Carr had had only one free throw coming, the referee would give the ball to the opposing team out-of-bounds. Since he has two shots coming, the referee will give Carr the ball again for his second try; the first is lost. If the distraction had come from one of the opposing players, it would be a different story—Carr would still get both free throws, *and* an additional throw for a technical foul by the opposing team.

14. The ball must hit the rim of the basket or the backboard within the allotted time. Anything else is considered a pass, not a legal shot.

THE GAME

Basketball has changed quite a bit since that afternoon in 1891 when Dr. James Naismith wrote the original rules—thirteen of them. Today's Official Rule Book of the N.B.A. consists of thirty pages of very fine print. But the durability of those original rules, and of the game itself, is quite a tribute to Dr. Naismith.

With only slight modifications, these six original rules of basketball have remained unchanged for more than eighty years:

1. The ball may be thrown in any direction with one or both hands.
2. The ball may be batted in any direction with one or both hands, but not with the fists.
3. A player cannot run with the ball.
4. The ball must be held by only the hands; the arms and body may not be used in holding it.
5. No shouldering, holding, pushing, tripping, or striking of an opponent, in any way, shall be allowed.
6. When the ball goes out-of-bounds, it shall be thrown back into the field of play. The thrower-in is allowed five seconds. If he holds the ball longer, it shall go to the opponent.

Dr. Naismith went on to prescribe court dimensions, time limits, and simple foul situations. Later that same day, two empty peach baskets were tied to a balcony railing about ten feet from the floor at opposite ends of the gymnasium. After a few minutes of explanation, eighteen young men played America's first basketball game. Their enthusiasm for the new sport spread quickly.

This simple beginning is probably the main reason for the game's durability. Basketball is easy to understand (though it isn't necessarily

easy to put the ball in the basket), and it can be played almost anywhere, with a bare minimum of equipment. All you need is a round ball and a basket . . . or an empty garbage can . . . or even a cardboard box. In rural and residential areas, a driveway often does double duty as a basketball court. And in crowded cities, tiny all-cement school playgrounds have been the breeding grounds of great stars.

In the 1930's, three major rule changes were made that streamlined basketball into the fast-paced game we know today. The five-man team was already standard: two forwards, two guards, and a center. But it had become the practice of most teams to position their tallest man under the basket and have his teammates feed the ball to him for all the shots. Since there was a jump ball after every score, the same tall man could control the tip and then resume his position under the basket. If a team didn't have at least one tall man, they might play for several minutes without even *touching* the ball.

Two rule changes helped to offset the tall man's advantage: the formation of the foul lane under the basket, and the elimination of the jump ball after every score.

The foul lane was originally an area 6 feet wide, under the basket, where no offensive player could remain for more than three seconds, *with or without the ball.* (In subsequent years, the foul lane was widened to 12 feet and then to the present 16 feet.)

And instead of a jump for possession after every score, the ball would be handed to the scored-upon team, evening their chance to make a score of their own.

The third rule change helped to put more emphasis on defensive play. The court was divided in half by establishing the center line. The team with the ball was allowed no more than ten seconds to advance the ball into their offensive half of the court. This confined most of the play to a smaller area, increasing the defensive team's chance of stealing the ball from the offense.

Since 1936, the basic rules of the game have remained the same, though numerous technical details have been added. As professional basketball grew in popularity, uniform standards were established that still hold true today:

The Ball

The basketball is round, with a weight of not less than 20 ounces and not more than 22 ounces, inflated to 7½–8½ pounds. A basketball for adult use (high school, college, and pro) has a circumference of not less than 29½ inches and not more than 30 inches. The home team must provide at least three such balls for any official game.

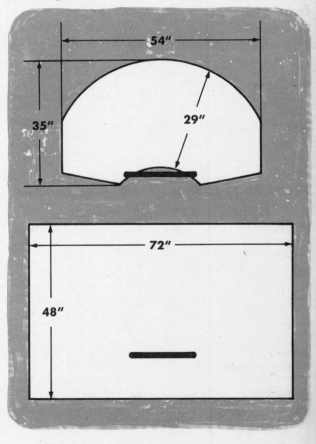

The Basket and Backboard

The basket at each end of the court is exactly 10 feet above the floor. It's 18 inches across and has a net which momentarily checks the progress of the ball when it passes through. The net is 15 to 18 inches long.

The basket ring is attached to a backboard. High schools use a fan-shaped backboard 54 inches by 35 inches. College and professional teams use a rectangular backboard 6 feet by 4 feet. The bottom of the backboard is exactly 9 feet above the floor, so the basket rim is a foot above the bottom of the backboard.

The ring of the basket is 6 inches from the face of the backboard. The face of the backboard is 4 feet in from the end line of the court, making the free throw line exactly 15 feet from the backboard.

The visiting team always selects the basket in which they will attempt to score during the first half of play. The teams change baskets at the beginning of the second half.

The Court

Although there are smaller ones at some high schools and in some gymnasiums, the legal pro basketball court is 50 feet wide and 94 feet long. The outside limits of the court are marked by a line 2 inches wide, and there should be at least 3 feet of clear space beyond the lines.

The length of the court is divided in half by the center line, or "ten-second line." At the exact center of the court is a 12-foot circle for center jumping. It is in this circle that the game periods are started with a jump ball.

At either end of the court, beneath the basket, there is a foul lane 16 feet wide and 19 feet long. At the end of this lane is another 12-foot circle. (When the foul lane was first established at 6 feet wide, the lane and the circle painted on the floor looked like an old-fashioned keyhole. That's why the area under the basket is called the "keyhole" or simply "the key," even though it no longer looks like one.)

Officials

Five officials oversee professional games; college and high school games require only four. There are two referees (one is sometimes called an umpire), a timer, and a scorer. In professional games, there's also a 24-second clock operator.

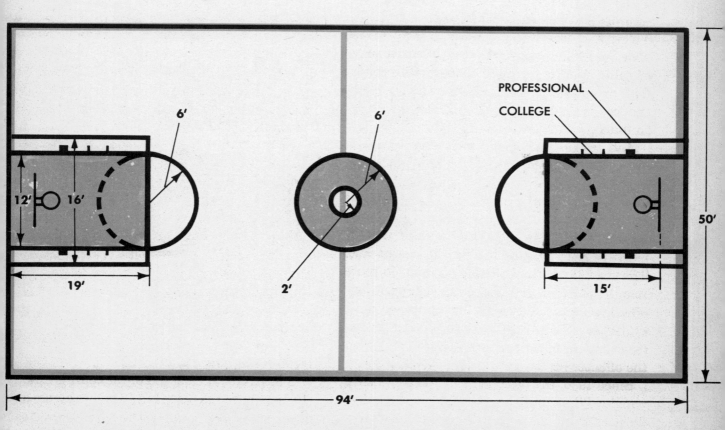

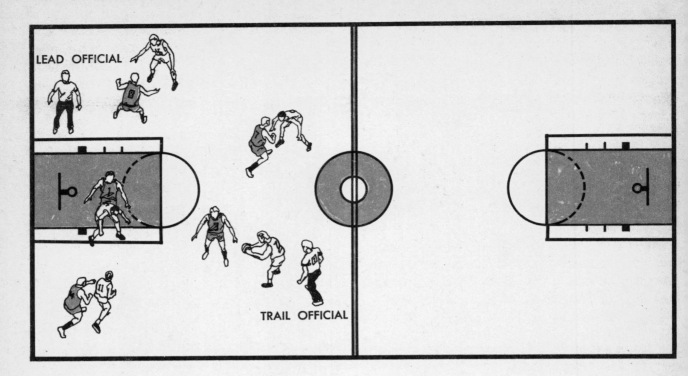

LEAD OFFICIAL

TRAIL OFFICIAL

Referees

The senior referee (the one with the most experience) is in charge of the game, and his word is final. He can, and does, make judgment calls for situations not specifically covered in the rules.

Before the game, the two referees inspect the game balls, the court, and the baskets, to make sure they meet N.B.A. standards. One of the referees will begin the game by throwing a jump ball in the center circle.

During the course of the play, one official always precedes the players in the direction of the offense, becoming the "lead official." The other follows behind both teams, becoming the "trail official." These roles reverse each time the direction of play changes.

One or both referees will blow a whistle and stop the play whenever a violation or foul is committed. They will signal the nature of the violation, or they will point to the player who committed the foul and then indicate how many free shots the fouled player is allowed. The official scorer records all this information in the game statistics.

Timer

This official starts and stops the game clock when signaled by the referees. When time ex- pires at the end of each period, he sounds a loud horn to end the play.

If the ball is in the air and heading toward the basket when the horn sounds, it will count as a score if it goes through, even though official playing time is over. That's why players will sometimes make a "desperation" full-court shot at the basket in the last seconds of a period or game. Once in a while, the result is spectacular!

During the third game of the 1970 play-offs between the Los Angeles Lakers and the New York Knicks, the Knicks were ahead by 2 points, with only four seconds left in the game. Jerry West—"Mr. Clutch"—took the throw-in pass under the Knicks' basket, dribbled twice, and shot for the Lakers' basket *63 feet away*. The game-ending horn sounded while the ball was in the air.

Swish! Under the Lakers' basket, Dave De-Busschere fell over backward watching the impossible shot drop cleanly through the basket. The roaring crowd had seen a record-breaking shot tie the score and throw the game into overtime.

(Unfortunately for the Lakers, they lost that game in the first overtime period. Jerry West went from depression to elation to depression, all in a few minutes—but that's basketball.)

24-Second Clock Operator

The 24-second rule was written into the books in 1954 to speed up professional basketball and prevent stalling. A team has twenty-four seconds (thirty seconds in the A.B.A.) in which to shoot for the basket once they've gained possession of the ball. If they don't get a shot off in that time, the ball is given to the other team.

The 24-second clocks are placed at the four corners of the playing floor, where they are visible to players, officials, and fans. The operator starts the 24-second clock when any member of a team gains possession of the ball. If an opponent knocks the ball out-of-bounds with less than ten seconds showing on the 24-second clock, the operator will reset the clock to ten seconds before the ball is put back into play.

Scorer

This official sits at the timing table and keeps a record of all field goals and free throws made and missed, plus personal and technical fouls called on each player and team. When a player has made six personal fouls, the scorer will immediately notify the referee, and that player will be ordered out of the game. The scorer also keeps track of the number of time-outs taken by each team and informs the referee when a team has used up all of its allotted time-outs.

If you want to keep track of game statistics yourself, these are the symbols used by basketball scorers:

2:	Field Goal
⊕:	Free Throw Made
Ov:	Free Throw Violation
Os:	Free Throw Substituted
OO:	Two-Shot Foul
QO or Q:	Bonus Opportunity
P1, P2, etc.:	Personal Foul
T1, T2:	Technical Foul

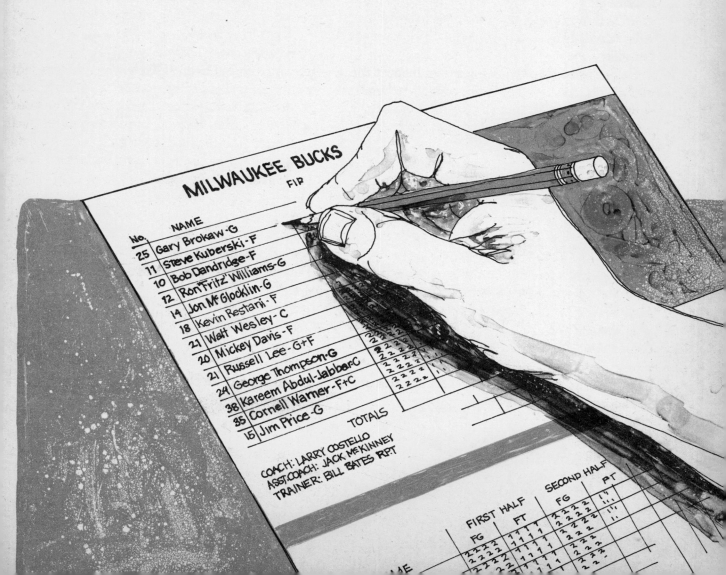

BASKETBALL RULES

Here's a simplified breakdown of the rules governing high school, college, and professional basketball:

Length of Game

High School—four periods of eight minutes each. Overtime periods of three minutes each.

College—two periods of twenty minutes each. Overtime periods of five minutes each.

Professional—four periods of twelve minutes each. Overtime periods of five minutes each.

Every period of play begins with a jump ball in the center circle. The referee throws the ball straight up between two players, and after the ball has reached its highest point, the players jump and attempt to tip or bat the ball to one of their teammates. Official game time does not begin until one of the jumpers touches the ball.

Time-Outs

High school and college—five time-outs of sixty seconds each.

Professional—seven time-outs of ninety seconds each.

Either team can call a time-out when the ball is dead. When the ball is in play, only the team with possession can call a time-out.

Professional teams are allowed a maximum of four time-outs in any of the first three periods, and only three time-outs in the last period. Each team *must* take at least one time-out per period. If they don't call for one, the referee will stop the game and make them take one. (This isn't so the players can rest. It's known as a "TV time-out," and it's used for commercials by the radio and television networks covering the game.)

24-Second Rule

The 24-second rule is, at present, used only by professional teams, though it has been considered for college use. A team must shoot for the basket within twenty-four seconds (thirty seconds in the A.B.A.) after gaining possession of the ball. If they fail to do so, the ball will be turned over to their opponents.

Scoring

At all levels, a field goal counts 2 points, and a foul shot counts 1 point. In the A.B.A. only, a field goal made 25 feet or farther from the basket counts 3 points.

Fouls and Free Throws

There are two types of fouls in basketball: personal and technical. Personal fouls are called against individual players who break the rules of the game during play. Technical fouls can be called against players, coaches, trainers, and even whole teams at any time—even during time-outs. Both types of fouls result in ball possession or free shots for the fouled team.

Here are some typical personal fouls:

1. When a player holds, pushes, or charges into another player or impedes the progress of another player by extending his arms or legs. When a player bends his body into any unnatural position to impede another player.

2. When a player makes excessive contact by use of his elbows.

3. When a dribbler charges into or contacts a defensive player in his path or tries to dribble through an area where an official feels there was not enough room. (This is an offensive foul.)

4. When a player forces a dribbler out of an established path of movement (unless the player can legally place himself in a defensive position first).

5. When a player who is screening (see p. 39) places himself closer than a normal step from his opponent, places himself to the side of or in front of a stationary opponent, makes any contact at all with the opponent, or even places himself so close to a moving opponent that the opponent cannot avoid contact by stopping or changing direction.

Technical fouls are called for unsportsmanlike conduct or for a number of other reasons, including delay of the game, too many timeouts, arguing with the officials, and even for hanging on the rim of the basket.

The number of free throws awarded to a team

that has been fouled depends on the type of foul, where it was committed, and how many other fouls have already been committed.

After a team has committed four defensive fouls in any period, the next fouls in that period will hurt them twice—on any foul beyond the fourth, the fouled player is allowed *two* tries to make his free throw. Once a team has committed four defensive fouls in any quarter, they are in the "penalty situation."

No free throws are awarded for offensive fouls, and these fouls count against individual players only. They do not add to the total of team fouls needed to put a team into the penalty situation. Possession of the ball is turned over to the fouled team at the sideline nearest where the foul was committed, and then play resumes.

One free throw is awarded for common rule-violation fouls.

Two free throws are awarded for common rule-violation fouls made in the backcourt (before the offensive team has taken the ball across the center line).

Two free throws are awarded for any foul committed against a player in the act of shooting for the basket.

In order to speed up professional basketball,

the first four common fouls in any period result only in change of possession. No free throws are awarded.

When a player is fouled and awarded a free throw, he takes a position at his team's free throw line to make his shot. Most players stand right behind the line in the center of the free throw circle, but some prefer to stand considerably farther back from the basket.

The free throw lanes on either side of the free throw line are occupied by other players as follows: One opposing team member stands on each lane closest to the basket. One of the shooter's teammates stands on either side of the lane next to the opposing players. One more opposing player can stand on either lane. All other players must keep at least 6 feet away from the free throw lanes.

When the shooter receives the ball from the referee, he must shoot his free throw within ten seconds. In the pros, the players on the lanes can move in for the rebound as soon as the ball leaves the shooter's hands. In high school and college, all players must hold their positions until the ball strikes the rim or backboard. If the free throw or throws are successful, the ball is given to the scored-upon team behind the end line, and play is resumed with a throw-in.

Most players use a one-handed set shot (see p. 32) for their free throws, but any type of shot may be used. Occasionally you'll see a player use an old-fashioned two-handed underhand toss. And Hal Greer, formerly of the Philadelphia 76ers, shot a jump shot from the free throw line!

One other important aspect of foul rules is this: If any individual player commits six fouls during the game (five in high school and college), he is disqualified from further play in that game; he's "fouled out."

Jump Balls

A jump ball is used to start each period of play. A jump ball is used when possession is disputed between two opposing players who are both touching the ball or when the ball is knocked out-of-bounds by two players at the same time. These same two players participate in the jump, regardless of any size difference. In all other jump situations, any two players may participate; usually the two tallest jump.

21

Here are some rules for jumpers:

1. Each jumper must have at least one foot (but may have both feet) inside the jumping circle, in the half of the circle which is farthest from his own basket.

2. The ball must be tapped by one or both of the jumpers after it reaches its highest point.

3. Neither jumper may touch the ball until it has reached its highest point.

4. Neither jumper may *catch* the tossed ball until one of the non-jumpers on the floor has touched it or until the ball has touched the floor, the basket, or the backboard.

5. Neither jumper may touch or tap the ball more than twice.

6. The eight non-jumpers must remain outside the restraining circle until the ball has been touched by one of the jumpers.

7. Teammates among the non-jumpers may not occupy adjacent spots around the circle if an opponent wants one of the spots.

Out-of-Bounds

A player is out-of-bounds if he steps over or touches anything on or outside the boundary lines marked on the floor. However, the position of a player in the air is determined by where he was last touching the floor. A player can leap out over the boundary line and still play the ball, as long as he remains in the air. Once he touches the floor out-of-bounds, he can no longer play the ball.

The ball is out-of-bounds if it touches a player or anything else outside the boundary lines. It's also out-of-bounds if it touches the supports or the back of the backboard, though it can, and sometimes does, roll along the top of the backboard and remain in play.

START CLOCK

JUMP BALL

BECKON
SUBSTITUTE

STOP
CLOCK

Officials' Signals

The referees use a set of hand signals to inform the scorer, timer, coaches, and fans of events during the game. When a player is fouled, the referee signals the type of foul, who committed it, and the number of free throws awarded. The referee will indicate with upheld fingers the number of points scored on a shot and, in the A.B.A., whether a shot is being attempted from the 3-point zone.

Here is a list of officials' signals (*not* in order of importance) and what they indicate:

Start Clock—This sharp, downward chop tells the timer to start the clock. On a throw-in, this signal will come at the instant the ball is touched by an inbounds player (not when the ball is *thrown*).

Stop Clock (Time-Out)—Arm up and hand open tells the timer to stop the clock.

Stop the Clock for a Jump Ball—Both fists out, thumbs up, mean that the official is calling for a jump ball and the clock should be stopped. Probably two opposing players were holding the ball or two players knocked the ball out-of-bounds simultaneously. The timer will automatically restart the game clock the moment the ball is touched during the jump.

Beckon Substitute—Any substitute player must check in at the timing table and then wait for an official on the floor to wave him into the game while the clock is stopped.

23

STOP
CLOCK—
FOUL

PUSHING

Stop the Clock for a Foul—A clenched fist held up tells the timer to stop the clock for a foul. Other signals will follow, indicating to the scorer what foul was committed, who committed it, and the number of free throws awarded.

Pushing or *Charging*—This action of pushing by an official indicates that a pushing or charging foul has been committed.

HOLDING

ILLEGAL
USE OF
HANDS

Holding—Holding is illegal, and this signal indicates an infraction of that rule. The official grasps his wrist and holds it so that the officials at the timing table can see it.

Illegal Use of Hands—The official brings the edge of one hand down in a sharp, chopping motion against his other wrist when he has spotted a player illegally using his hands to impede an opposing player.

TECHNICAL
FOUL

Technical Foul—The official forms a T with his hands to indicate a technical foul.

NO SCORE

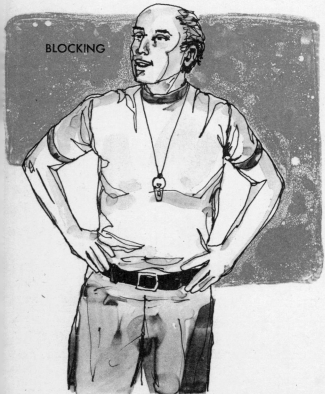

BLOCKING

Blocking—A player is not allowed to block or impede the progress of an opponent. If he does, the official will signal the infraction by placing both hands on his hips.

No Score—No team likes to see the official wave his arms in front of him, indicating that a basket does not count. If the offensive team commits a foul, such as offensive goaltending (see p. 12), as their basket is being made, the score will not be counted. Possession of the ball will be turned over to the opposing team.

25

SCORE
COUNTS

Score Counts (and Number of Points)—You'll see this signal after each successful field goal or free throw, and sometimes even when the ball does *not* go through the hoop. If the defensive team is guilty of defensive goaltending, their opponents will be awarded a score even though the ball was batted away from the basket.

3-POINT
SHOT
(A.B.A.)

Shot from the 3-Point Zone—In the A.B.A. only, this signal indicates that a shot from beyond 25 feet out is successful and that 3 points are to be awarded.

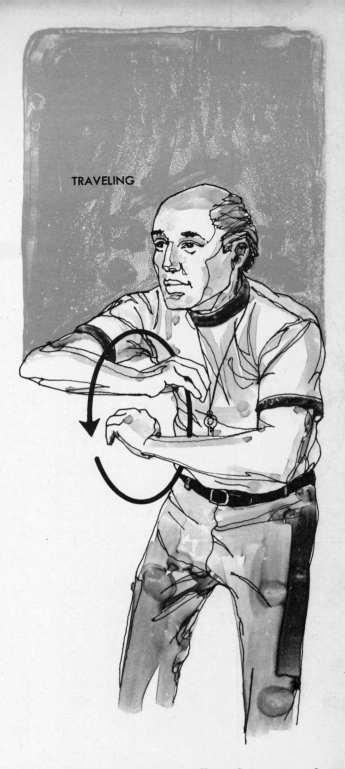

TRAVELING

Traveling—No player is allowed to *carry* the ball from one point on the floor to another; he must dribble (see p. 29). When any player receives the ball, he's allowed to take only one step in any direction without dribbling, or two steps if in the act of shooting. (If he receives the ball while in the air and lands on both feet at once, he's still allowed one step.) When an official rotates both fists in front of his chest, he's signaling that the player in possession has taken more than one step without dribbling. Since this is a violation, no free throws are awarded, but possession is given to the opposing team.

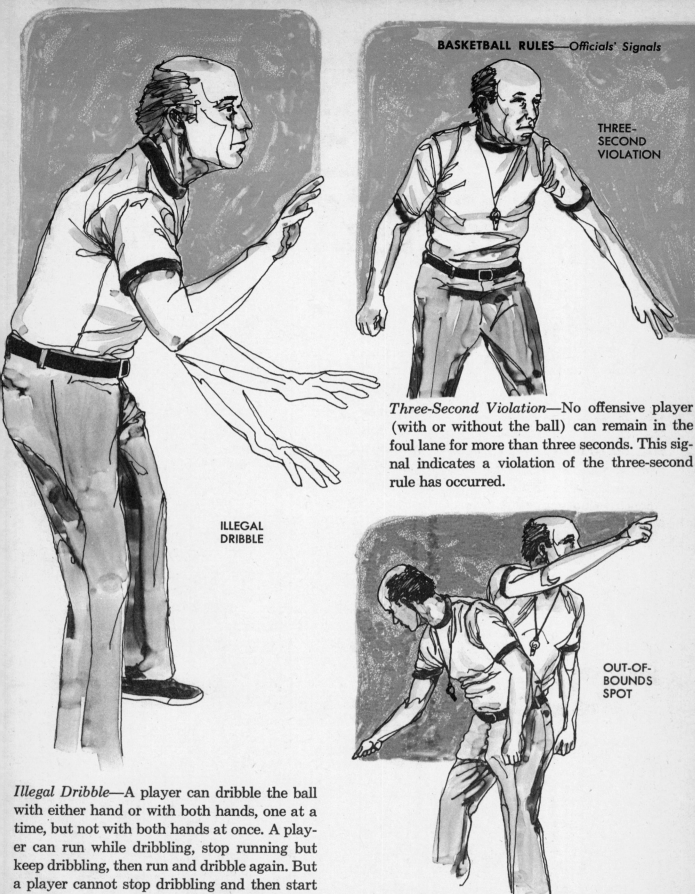

THREE-
SECOND
VIOLATION

Three-Second Violation—No offensive player (with or without the ball) can remain in the foul lane for more than three seconds. This signal indicates a violation of the three-second rule has occurred.

ILLEGAL
DRIBBLE

OUT-OF-
BOUNDS
SPOT

Illegal Dribble—A player can dribble the ball with either hand or with both hands, one at a time, but not with both hands at once. A player can run while dribbling, stop running but keep dribbling, then run and dribble again. But a player cannot stop dribbling and then start dribbling again. Nor can a player "carry" the ball by putting his hand beneath it during the dribble. A dribbling-motion signal by the official indicates that the player in possession has broken one of the rules of dribbling. This, too, is a violation.

Out-of-Bounds Spot—This signal will be given after violations that result in a change of possession, to indicate the spot where the ball will be taken out-of-bounds for a throw-in. It's also an indication of which direction the ball will be moving when play resumes.

27

CHAPTER

5

THE BASIC SKILLS

In some other sports, like football, there's a lot of room for specialization. If you happen to be a great kicker, that's all you'll have to do—kick. If you happen to be particularly quick and agile, you may do nothing but return kick-offs. Whatever your skill, you will specialize in offense or defense, and while the other squad is doing its thing on the field, you'll be resting on the bench.

Not so in basketball. Naturally, ball-handling and shooting skills will vary from man to man, but in basketball, each individual has to be able to do it all . . . on offense and defense. Shooting may be your biggest problem—but if you're in the best position to shoot, you've got to shoot. Maybe you're weakest in passing—but if you've got the ball and one of your teammates is set up, you've got to pass. You probably don't like the idea of getting a face full of elbow under the backboard—but if the rebound is there waiting for you, you've got to go for it.

It takes a lot more than just height to make a basketball player. Nate Archibald of the Kansas City Kings and Calvin Murphy of the Houston Rockets aren't even six feet tall. They didn't get to be superstars because of size but because of skill.

The basic skills of basketball are easy to understand, and most of them are not too difficult to learn to do. Once you've learned them, it's up to you how much polish and practice you put into them. Like any other skills, they take time. But, unlike some others, basketball skills can be fun.

Dribbling
One way a player in possession moves the ball from place to place is by dribbling—quickly bouncing the ball along beside or in front of him—or even *behind* him—as he advances downcourt. Any player in possession is allowed to take only one step without dribbling.

A player cannot start, stop, and then start his dribble again. He cannot charge into another player while dribbling. He cannot dribble with both hands at once, though he can *alternate* hands.

Generally, a high, slow bounce is used for a long move down the court and a low, fast bounce for accuracy and better ball control in tight situations.

The dribble ends when the player allows the ball to stop bouncing, or when he touches it with both hands at once, or when he loses control of it.

Actually, generally speaking, the less the ball is dribbled the better. In high school and college games, where stalling is permitted, dribbling is often used just to kill time. But this is dangerous—the ball can be stolen from even the best dribbler.

A good dribbler alternates from one hand to

the other to keep the ball from a defender, using his body as a shield between the defender and ball. He'll feint or fake a move in one direction, then dribble in another direction, leaving the defender reaching for thin air.

A common mistake, even with some pros, is to dribble automatically immediately after receiving the ball. Remember: even *one bounce* counts as a dribble, and once you've used it up you can't start again. Don't dribble the ball just to be doing something with it. Plan your dribble so that it takes the ball where you want it to go.

Practice dribbling standing still to get the "feel" of the ball, and get used to dribbling with either hand. Then try moving around while dribbling. You'll know when you've got dribbling mastered—when you can dribble from one place to another, alternating hands, *without ever looking at the ball*.

Passing

The ball can be moved in any direction and for any distance by passing from one player to another. There's more to passing than just tossing the ball back and forth, since whenever the ball is in the air between players, there's a danger of its being grabbed by an opponent.

The most common basketball pass is the *two-handed chest snap*. The ball is held in both hands in front of the player's chest and flipped or snapped directly to another player. This works fine as long as there's nobody between the passer and the receiver.

A *bounce pass* is often used to get the ball past an opponent and to a teammate. The ball can be thrown from a chest snap or one-handed from either hand, but it's caromed (bounced once) off the floor to the receiver instead of thrown directly to him. This isn't as easy as it may sound; the ball must be delivered with just the right speed and *spin*, or it will bounce off the floor too high or low. The ball should have a slight forward spin in the direction of the receiver.

TWO-HANDED CHEST SNAP

BOUNCE PASS

A two-handed *overhead pass* is often used to get the ball over a defender or to a taller receiver, especially in the key area, where players are crowded together. The ball is held in both hands above the thrower's head and thrown with a snap of the forearms and wrists.

A one-handed *baseball pass* is sometimes used to throw the ball the entire length of the court to an open man. Since this pass must be thrown hard, control is difficult. Just like a baseball, a basketball will curve in flight if there's a sidespin on it. To avoid sidespin, let the ball roll straight off your fingertips, with your palm down, fingers pointing toward the receiver.

Practice passing and receiving with a friend, varying the speed and distance. When you practice bounce passes, make sure the surface you're on is relatively level. Experiment with putting a little spin on the ball to see how it might help, or *hurt*, you in a game passing situation.

OVERHEAD PASS

BASEBALL PASS

Shooting

The only real way to master shooting is to practice and then practice some more, with a full-sized basketball and a regulation-height basket and backboard. Vary the angle and distance, and try for some consistency with different types of shots. It's no good to become an expert at only one type of shot—you may never have a chance to use it in a game.

Regardless of the type of shot, shooting requires coordinated movement of the entire body, not just the hands and arms. In actual play, there is rarely time (except at the free throw line) to get into a stance, take a breath, relax, aim, and shoot the ball. Watch how professionals "flow" into a shot in one smooth, continuous movement.

Sometimes, players aim for the backboard directly above the hoop and bank their shots through. Other times, they aim dead center for the basket. The angle of the shot determines which is preferable. Try both methods from various positions on the floor; use the one that's most effective for you, from a given position on the floor.

In the *one-handed set shot*, the ball is held at eye level, cradled in the palm of the non-shooting hand. The fingertips of the shooting hand rest against the back of the ball. The foot corresponding to the shooting hand should be in front of the other foot; both knees should be slightly flexed. The shot is lined up *through* the shooting arm all the way to the elbow, which should always point down and be held close to the body prior to shooting. The ball is shot with a straightening of the legs and a push from the shooting arm.

ONE-HANDED SET SHOT

The *two-handed set shot* is similar except that the ball is held and pushed with both hands. For many players, this shot is not as accurate as the one-handed shot. Since most people tend to be stronger in one arm than in the other, the ball might fly off at an angle. However, an expert at this shot can be deadly accurate.

The *jump shot* is the most widely used shot in basketball today. When properly executed, it's a beautiful shot. It begins with a position similar to that of the one-handed set shot, but with a deeper bend of the knees for more spring. All in one movement, the shooter straightens his legs and raises the ball above his head, so that the elbow of the shooting arm is at eye level. The ball is shot with a snap of the wrist. The height of the jump isn't the most important factor of this shot, unless the shooter is closely guarded. Some shooters jump only a few inches off the floor, others two feet or more. It *is* important to shoot exactly at the top of the jump, so that the ball has the momentum of the entire body behind it.

JUMP SHOT

Basketball's most difficult shot (to shoot *and* to defend against) is the *hook shot*. The hook is difficult to shoot because the shooter must begin this shot "blind"—with his back to the basket. It's difficult to defend against because the shooter always has his body between the ball and the defender.

The shooter begins by holding the ball in both hands at chest level, crouching slightly. His defender and the basket are both behind him. In one continuous movement, the shooter straightens and pivots on the foot opposite the shooting hand, extending his shooting arm so that his body remains between the defender and the ball. As the basket comes into the shooter's sight, the ball is shot, with a wide, sweeping arc of the arm, up and over the shooter's (and the defender's) head. Many players incorporate a jump into the hook shot for extra height over the defender. When Kareem Abdul-Jabbar (7 feet 2) delivers his jumping hook shot, the sportscasters call it the "skyhook." It is virtually unstoppable.

HOOK SHOT

The _lay-up shot_ is the end result of a successful drive play—when a player has broken free and rushed in under the basket. In a sense, the lay-up isn't really a shot at all, since the ball isn't _thrown_ toward the basket. With a high jump, the shooter gets up as close as possible to the basket and lets the ball roll off his hand and through the hoop. Most lay-up shots require some excellent dribbling first, in order for the shooter to get the ball in close for the jump. If the drive is straight to the basket, the ball is usually dropped through the hoop. From an angle, it's usually banked gently off the backboard.

You'll see the _dunk_ or _stuff shot_ only in professional basketball, since it's illegal in high school and college play. This is the tall player's shot, used regularly by Wilt Chamberlain, for-

merly of the Los Angeles Lakers, and other tall superstars. From a position close under the basket, the shooter jumps straight up and stuffs the ball through the hoop with a one- or two-handed slam. As mentioned earlier in the book, there's a rule against _goaltending,_ or touching the ball when it is in flight directly above the basket. But during a dunk shot, at least according to pro rules, the ball is never really in flight—it's in the shooter's possession until the instant it goes through the hoop!

DUNK SHOT

LAY-UP SHOT

Rebounding

In actual play, one of the most important aspects of basketball is the ability to gain control of the ball when it rebounds off the backboard or rim after a missed shot. A player under his own basket usually attempts to tip the ball back into the basket for a score (the *tip-in shot*). An opposing player attempts to gain possession and get the ball to one of his teammates for a try at their own basket.

Basketball pros refer to the area directly under the basket as "the butcher shop." The roughest part of the game takes place there—sometimes as many as eight men struggling to control the ball in an area about six feet wide.

Offensive rebounding can help a team that's weak in shooting by giving each shot two or three chances to go through the hoop. Normally the offensive center and two forwards try to tip in their team's missed shots. Sometimes a

team will "crash" the backboard by sending all five players after rebounds. This gets crowded, and it's dangerous strategy, since it leaves all of the opposing players unguarded against a fast break.

Offensive rebounding may be somewhat simpler than defensive, since it takes only one hand to tip or push the ball back into the hoop. But offensive rebounders must be careful not to take wild slaps at the ball, control being still essential.

Defensive rebounding is plain hard work. A defensive rebounder usually has to use both hands, since he's not only trying to keep the

ball from going through the hoop but also trying to gain possession of it. Since defensive players take positions between the offense and the basket, they're in closer for rebounds, and they try to keep it that way. Defenders will "screen off the boards" or "box out" offensive players who are trying for rebounds. They do this by taking up as much of the limited space under the basket as they can, with elbows, legs, and bottoms. If the defensive rebounder gains possession of the ball, he tries as quickly as possible to make an "outlet pass" to a teammate, who may have a clear path for a drive play and a lay-up at the other end of the court. Teams that are especially good at defensive rebounding, like the Los Angeles Lakers, sometimes use a technique called "cherry picking." In this play, as soon as the battle for a rebound begins, one of the defensive players drops back, sometimes as far as the center line. If one of his teammates gets the rebound and passes the ball to him, he's already halfway to his own basket.

In crowded rebounding situations, fouls can and do occur easily. But there's an "incidental contact" rule in pro basketball. This means that when players are making a legal and legitimate attempt to gain possession of a loose ball, they can slam and bump one another without fouling. The judgment of the officials will determine when fouls are called during rebounding.

In a rebounding situation, the ball is "loose" —neither team has possession. Fouls committed when the ball is loose—"loose ball fouls"— result in possession for the fouled team. No free throws are awarded.

CHAPTER 6

STRATEGY:
OFFENSE AND DEFENSE

As in many competitive sports, there's some controversy in basketball over the relative importance of defense and offense. Strictly speaking, of course, good defense doesn't win basketball games. But most coaches today give equal weight to defensive play and offensive play. A lot of coaches go even further and say, "If you're going to relax, relax on *offense*—not defense!"

Originally, basketball was predominantly a game of offense. Individual players, especially in the pros, developed fantastic ball-handling and shooting skills. As these skills became more or less uniform throughout the leagues, coaches realized that they would have to counteract them with some equally fantastic defense. Defensive basketball caught up fast. One thing you *won't* see nowadays is a team hanging back on defense, resting and saving their energy for the time when they get the ball.

Offense or defense—do you think one is more important than the other? Remember that basketball players have to change back and forth, often in the blink of an eye. Think it over as

you read about some of the basics of both offense and defense.

BASIC OFFENSE

There are two types of offense in basketball: the *fast break* and the *set* type. Both can be used to advantage, though fans generally prefer the more exciting fast break.

In the set offense, used primarily in high school and college, plays follow predetermined patterns. Each player has a specific route to a specific place on the floor. One particular player is assigned to shoot from a set spot at a set time, and all the other players have special duties designed to help the shooter get to the right spot. Some teammates will set up *picks* by standing in the path of the defensive player following the dribbler. Since no moving player is allowed to run into a stationary player, the defender will have to change his course.

Part of the play might call for a *switch*. This is accomplished by having the dribbler and a teammate quickly cross each other's paths while their defenders are close. In order to keep

SWITCH AND MISMATCH

from colliding, the defenders have to stop following the man they were assigned to guard. If a switch results in a smaller defender guarding a taller offensive player, the result is a *mismatch*, and it forces the defenders to change their strategy.

At the right moment, one or more players might be assigned to *screen* the shooter by positioning themselves between him and the defense, giving him room and time to make his shot while temporarily unguarded.

One of the difficulties with a set offensive

play is that it takes time. The longer one team maneuvers with the ball, the better are the chances for the other team to steal it—and if one individual forgets his assignment or fails to carry it out, the whole play might be ruined.

Fast break is the name of the game the professionals play. There are several reasons for this. One is simply that the fans pay to see lots of fast-paced action. Also, pro defense has become so specialized that teams can't afford to take the time to run set pattern plays. The fast break just means their getting the ball down the court and into the basket in a hurry, before the defense has time to react.

Another reason is the 24-second clock. Pro teams have only twenty-four seconds to shoot for the basket after gaining possession of the ball. There isn't time for a lot of fancy pattern work to get the ball into shooting range.

Finally, high school and college teams may have to plan their whole offense around one excellent dribbler and one excellent shooter. The pros don't have that problem—every player on a pro team is a potential scorer.

The fast break offense requires skill and teamwork. Picks and switches and screens are still used, but instead of following specific assignments, the pros *free-lance*. Each player does whatever he can to get the ball into the best position for a shot. Whoever ends up with the clearest chance to make the basket will shoot for it, even though he may not be the team's best shooter.

Fast break basketball is exciting to watch. It has been rumored, in fact, that the National Collegiate Athletic Association is considering a 24-second rule, or some variation of it, to speed up college basketball.

FAST BREAK

BASIC DEFENSE

There are two types of defense in basketball: *man-to-man* and *zone.* In high school and college, coaches can select either type or switch back and forth, depending on the situation on the court. In the pros, using a zone defense is against the rules. (There's nothing wrong or bad about zone defense itself. But it does tend to slow down the action on the floor, and some professional rules, such as the one against zone defense, were made to speed up the game.) A technical foul is called against a pro team for using a zone defense.

In the basic defensive stance, a player faces his opponent with his arms and hands out, his feet apart, his knees flexed, and his weight evenly distributed. From this position, a defender can move quickly in any direction to block a move by his opponent. The defender can position himself as close as possible to the front or side of his opponent as long as no contact is made. If he's behind an opponent, he must keep at least one step away. The rules say that once a defender assumes this position, he cannot move *toward* his opponent, but only in the same direction his opponent moves (or in the direction he *thinks* his opponent will move).

As suggested by the name, the man-to-man defense is set up so that each defender always guards an individual player on the offensive team. There will be times when a defensive player will have to switch and guard another player—when offensive players cross paths or set picks, for example.

The defending player always attempts to remain between the man he's guarding and the basket. He harasses his man with arm waving, crowding, and even touching, which is legal so long as it does not impede the opponent's progress. He tries to block passes to and from his man and, of course, shots attempted by his man. If the offensive player is dribbling near a boundary line, the defender will try to force him out-of-bounds.

In a zone defense, the defensive players align themselves on the floor in a preset pattern, or formation. Each man becomes responsible for the *area* he is in, rather than for any particular offensive player. Each defensive area is aligned so that it touches the next area and the whole front court is covered.

DEFENSIVE STANCE

HARASSING

41

Defensive guarding techniques are similar to those in the man-to-man type of defense. But each time *any* offensive player enters a particular zone, the defensive player responsible for that zone guards him until he leaves it.

As mentioned before, a zone defense tends to slow down the offense by forcing them to spend more time setting up their shots. Zones have their weaknesses, too. A defender might be in the wrong part of his zone to block a pass or shot from that zone.

Both types of defense can be *tight* or *loose*, depending on the preference of the coach and the game situation.

In a tight, or *pressing*, defense, the defending players guard their men as physically closely as possible and as soon as possible after the opposition has gained possession. The defenders begin their harassing techniques even before the offensive team has taken the ball across the center line—a backcourt press. (Remember that the offensive team has only ten seconds to get the ball across the center line; otherwise, it will lose possession.)

In a loose defense, the defending players take their positions under the offensive team's basket, without a backcourt press, and they don't get as physically close to the men they're guarding. Using both types of defense alternately, teams try to throw their opponents off guard.

TIGHT DEFENSE

42

CHAPTER 7

PUTTING IT ALL TOGETHER

Take the basic skills, mix in some offensive and defensive strategy, add ten players . . . and you've got the potential for some of the fastest action in sports.

Most coaches try to season this recipe with just the right combination of height, speed, and ability in their players. When all the ingredients are blended properly, the result is beautiful basketball.

Positions

The five players on a basketball team generally take the same positions on offense and defense, usually guarding the man corresponding to their position on their own team.

The two *forwards* cover the area near the corners of the court on either side of the basket. Their job is to score and to rebound. Ideally, one forward should be a super-shooter; the other a super-rebounder.

The *center*, often called the "pivot man," plays near the basket. The center is almost always the tallest player on the team. He must be an excellent shooter *and* rebounder. He also has the important job of coordinating the efforts of his team. The center spends much of his time with his back to the basket, watching his teammates and their defenders, and "feeding" the ball to a teammate who has a clear shot at the basket.

Some centers take a "low post" position, close to the basket, on one side of the foul lane. Other centers prefer a "high post" position, farther from the basket, near the top of the free throw

HIGH POST

LOW POST

circle. Whether to use a high post or low post position is frequently determined by the defensive capabilities of the opposing center. Teams will frequently choose the high post, for example, against a team with a seven-foot-plus pivot man, to keep him farther away from the basket, where his rebounding and shot-blocking potential is most dangerous. They will tend to favor the low post when the *offensive* center has the height advantage.

The two *guards* cover the area toward the middle of the court. Guards are often the shortest players on the team and fast movers. One guard should be an excellent outside shooter; the other is sometimes a "driver" who can move in toward the basket for a quick lay-up if there's an opening.

PUTTING IT TOGETHER ON OFFENSE

Faking a Defender—In every one-on-one situation, it's the job of the ball handler to get around the man guarding him, in order to pass or to get a clear shot at the basket. To do this, he must be able to outmaneuver his guard. You'll see this in every basketball game.

Frequently a player who has received the ball holds it momentarily as he studies the situation. The man guarding him will have taken a defensive stance to the front or side. If the ball

handler decides to make a break for the basket, to shoot or pass, he must first get around his guard. So he'll make a *jab-step* to the right with his right foot, causing his guard to shift momentarily in that direction. Instead of going to the right, the ballcarrier crosses his right foot over in front of his left and dribbles around the guard, to the left.

When the offensive player has the ball within shooting range, his defender will be between him and the basket, trying to block a shot or pass. A *head-and-shoulder fake* by the offensive player might fool the defender into raising his arms or jumping to block a shot. The offensive player can easily pass the ball around him or wait and shoot a jumper as the defender is coming back down.

JAB STEP

The Guard-Around Move—In this maneuver, the guard passes to the forward, who has faked to free himself and moved forward to receive the pass. The guard then fakes a move to the inside, using the jab-step or a head and shoulder fake. But he actually goes outside and gets a return pass from the forward. The guard then uses the forward to screen his defender out of the way while he drives for a shot.

The Give-and-Go—Once again, the forward fakes to free himself and receives a pass from the guard. The guard fakes to the outside, drives inside, and receives a return pass from the forward for an easy shot.

Splitting the Post—This maneuver can be used by both guards or by a guard and a forward, depending on the position of the center. If the center is in the high post position, the guard with the ball passes to him, and then both guards take their defensive men straight toward the baseline. When they have backed their defenders far enough to use the center as a screen, the guards will cut around the center,

and the guard who passed will get the ball back for a shot. If one of the defenders gets suspicious and refuses to back up, the guard he's covering can fake around and go straight to the basket on a give and go from the center.

If the center is in the low post position, he can receive a pass from either the guard or the forward. The guard and forward then fake away from the center but instead drive toward him and cross in front of him, using him to screen off their defenders.

In both of these maneuvers, it should always be the player who passed the ball to the center who crosses in front of him first.

Pick and Roll—This is one of the oldest and most effective moves in basketball. Here, one player stands stationary to pick the defender away from the dribbler, pivots around after the dribbler has gone by him, and drives toward the basket to receive a pass from the dribbler, who is momentarily unguarded. The secret in this play is for the pick man to pivot and move without taking his eyes off the ball. The pick

GUARD AROUND

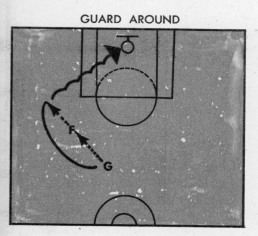

GIVE AND GO

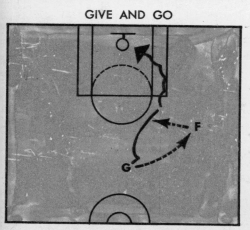

SPLITTING THE POST

PICK AND ROLL

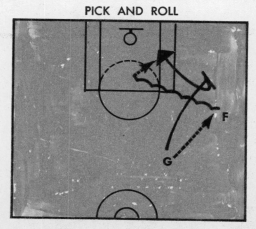

and roll can be worked by the guards, a guard and a forward, a guard and the center, or a forward and the center.

Most offensive plays, whether they're planned or free-lanced, involve two or three players. What about the others? They act as decoys and keep their defenders out of the way of the real action. It's always the job of each offensive player to get the ball into the best position for a shot, even if it means "sacrificing" an opportunity to get some attention with a flashy—but chancy—shot of his own.

PUTTING IT TOGETHER ON DEFENSE

Learn the Opponent's Moves—Naturally, a defender expects the player he's guarding to fake in order to move the ball. So, in one-on-one situations, it's important for a player to study the moves of the man he's been assigned to guard. With which hand does he prefer to dribble? What fancy moves does he have? What's his best shot—and from what particular spot? If the offensive player dribbles mostly with his right hand, the defender will be wary of fakes to the left. If his best shot is a jumper from the right of the basket, the defender should be prepared to block it . . . or better yet, keep him away from the spot from which he shoots it.

The Wasted Jump—Here's another thing a defender should watch out for. The player he's guarding receives the ball and fakes an overhead pass or a jump shot. If the defender jumps up to block the ball, the offensive player can easily dribble around him and get away. A good defensive player will never jump unless his man has *used up his dribble*. (Remember that a player with the ball can dribble only once.

WASTED JUMP

BLOCKING THE CENTER

HEAD AND SHOULDER FAKE

He must remain wherever he stops dribbling until he gets rid of the ball.)

Blocking the Center—Against many teams, it is imperative that the defense concentrate on blocking the center. Trying to contain such a man, especially if he is tall and accurate, is a tough job. Often the defense will align to block passes to the center rather than try to stop him from shooting.

The man specifically assigned to guard the center should play alongside him and slightly in front. As the ball is being passed among the offense, the defender should shift to block passes. Meanwhile, one or more defensemen align themselves more toward the center by *sagging* or *collapsing* off their own assignments.

This does uncover other offensive players somewhat, but the idea is to blanket the center and force the offense to take more difficult shots.

Play the Ball—There comes a time when every good defensive player feels he has an excellent chance to steal the ball from the dribbler. This is a tricky process that can easily result in a foul. But a successful steal is an exhilarating way (and humiliating for the opposition!) of gaining possession. Since a good dribbler will always try to keep his body between the ball and the man who's defending against him, it's often another defensive player who makes the steal, from the open side. Before attempting a steal, the defender should consider the foul situation. How many personals does he have? Is his team in the penalty situation? Is a steal worth the risk of giving the dribbler a chance at the free throw line? (Maybe the dribbler is a terrible free throw shooter.)

The safest way to steal the ball and avoid a foul is for the defender to stick his hand in low

STEALING

47

2-1-2 ZONE

as the ball is bouncing up from the floor during a dribble, bounce it once, out of the way of the dribbler, and continue the dribble in the opposite direction. (Remember the rules of dribbling: Once the defender has bounced the ball, he cannot stop bouncing it and then start again.)

An easy lay-up is the hoped-for result of a stolen dribble.

Zone Defense—Not legal in the pros (but used in spite of this, if they feel they can get away with it), zone defense is still a part of the basketball played by high schools and colleges. In this type of defense, a defender is responsible for a specific area of the floor rather than a specific player. He guards any offensive player who enters his zone.

There are several different formations that teams can take to form zone defenses. Where the defender stations himself within his zone

2-2-1 ZONE

1-2-2 ZONE

depends on where the ball is on the court and where the offensive players are. Illustrated are the 2-1-2 zone, the 1-2-2 zone, the 2-2-1 zone, and the 1-3-1 zone.

The coach will select the type of zone, depending on the height and speed of his own players and the offensive abilities of the other team. Generally speaking, the coach would like to see as many defensemen as possible between the ball and the basket.

The Zone Press—This defense is the specialty of the U.C.L.A. basketball team. The players establish their zones in the backcourt as soon as the opposition gains possession, then move the zones right along with the ball. The offense is under constant harassment from the moment the ball is in play. Each defender, within his zone, positions himself as close as possible to the ball, pressuring the offense to pass rather than dribble—thus making it easier to steal.

1-3-1 ZONE

Devise Your Own Plays

Use ten squares of red and blue paper for the players. Identify each position with its abbreviation on the player square: F, C, G. Use a bottle cap for the ball, and move your players around the court in various formations. Use certain players to pick and screen other players.

But remember: The idea is to make a score or at least draw a foul. There's no percentage in beautiful ball handling and playmaking if the result is not a score.

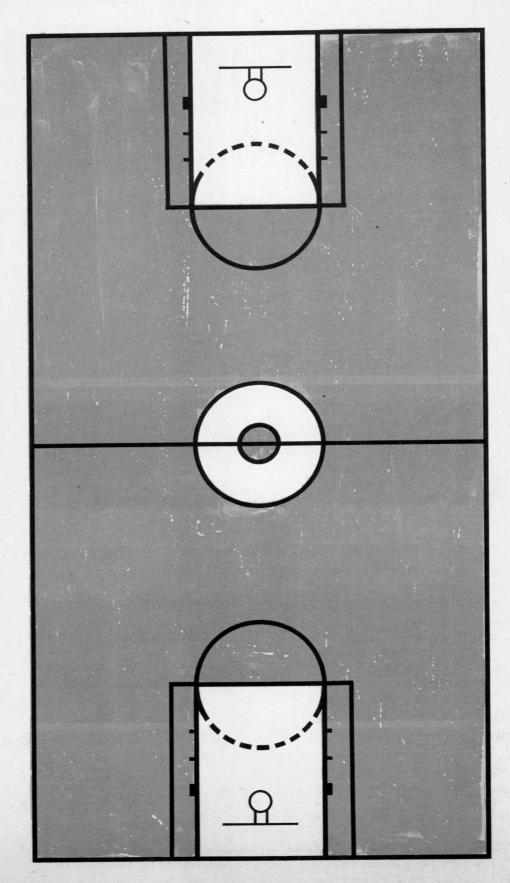

CHAPTER 8

RECORDS AND THE HALL OF FAME

When Dr. Naismith put down his original rules for moving the ball and scoring, he could not anticipate the high degree of skill that future players would develop at dribbling, passing, and shooting. Basketball is one of the few popular sports in which several rule changes have *had* to be made to keep up with the rapid increase in player skills. The fast-paced action of today's basketball represents an excellent balance of playing rules and player skills.

Since the founding of the National Basketball Association in 1949, professional basketball has had numerous superstars. One name in particular—Wilt Chamberlain—stands out in today's records . . . but, after all, records are for breaking.

Here are some of the outstanding statistics of professional basketball, courtesy of the N.B.A.:

FIELD GOALS

All-time field goal leader: Wilt Chamberlain, 12,681, Philadelphia, San Francisco, Los Angeles, 1960–1973

Season field goal leader: Wilt Chamberlain, 1,597, Philadelphia, 1961–62

Single-game field goal leader: Wilt Chamberlain, 36, Philadelphia vs. New York, 1962

FREE THROWS

All-time free throw leader: Oscar Robertson, 7,694, Cincinnati, Milwaukee, 1961–73

Season free throw leader: Jerry West, 840, Los Angeles, 1966

Single-game free throw leader: Wilt Chamberlain, 28, Philadelphia vs. New York, 1962

SCORING
All-time scoring leader: Wilt Chamberlain, 31,419

Season scoring leader: Wilt Chamberlain, 4,029, Philadelphia, 1962

Single-game scoring leader: Wilt Chamberlain, 100, Philadelphia vs. New York, 1962

ASSISTS
All-time leader, assists: Oscar Robertson, 9,887

Season leader, assists: Nate Archibald, 910, Kansas City, 1973

Single-game leader, assists: Bob Cousy, 28, Boston vs. Minneapolis, 1959; Guy Rodgers, 28, San Francisco vs. St. Louis, 1963

REBOUNDS
All-time leader, rebounds: Wilt Chamberlain, 23,924

Season leader, rebounds: Wilt Chamberlain, 2,149, Philadelphia, 1961

Single-game leader, rebounds: Wilt Chamberlain, 55, Philadelphia vs. Boston, 1960

PERSONAL FOULS
All-time leader, personal fouls: Hal Greer, 3,855, Syracuse, Philadelphia, 1959–73

Season leader, personal fouls: Bill Bridges, 366, St. Louis, 1968

The Naismith Hall of Fame in Springfield, Massachusetts, opened in February of 1968. Unlike its counterparts in other sports, the Naismith Hall of Fame honors contributors and players at all levels: professional, military, collegiate, and high school. The thirteen-member Honors Committee annually selects enshrinees from four categories—players, coaches, contributors, and referees.

Four complete teams are also enshrined in the Hall of Fame. They are the "First Team"; the Original Celtics; The Buffalo, N.Y., Germans; and the New York Renaissance ("Rens").

There's a fascinating array of basketball memorabilia on display, including a life-size replica of the gymnasium in which the game was first played. Enshrined in the Honors Room are the following individuals, listed in the order in which they were elected:

(Courtesy of the Naismith Memorial Hall of Fame)

JAMES NAISMITH, M.D., inventor of the game in 1891

OSWALD TOWER, *contributor,* member of the Official Rules Committee, 1910–59; editor of *Basketball Guide,* 1915–59

RALPH MORGAN, *contributor,* founder of the Collegiate Rules Committee, 1905

JOHN J. SCHOMMER, *college player,* University of Chicago, 1907–09; led Western Conference in scoring all three years; made an 80-foot field goal to win the national title game in 1908

FORREST C. ("PHOG") ALLEN, *contributor,* founder, National Association of Basketball Coaches (N.A.B.C), 1927

HENRY C. CARLSON, M.D., *coach,* University of Pittsburgh, 1922–53; led Pitt teams to National Championships in 1928 (an undefeated season) and 1930

LUTHER H. GULICK, M.D., *contributor,* Physical Training Chairman, Springfield, Mass., Y.M.C.A.; asked Dr. Naismith to create a "new indoor sport" in 1891

EDWARD J. HICKOX, *contributor,* President, N.A.B.C., 1944–46

CHARLES D. HYATT, *college player,* University of Pittsburgh, 1928–30; the nation's leading scorer in 1930; set college record of 880 points

MATTHEW P. KENNEDY, *referee,* high school, collegiate, and professional official, 1928–46; Supervisor of Officials in the National Basketball Association, 1946–50

ANGELO LUISETTI, *college player,* Stanford University, 1936–38; twice all-American; pioneer of the one-handed set shot

WALTER E. MEANWELL, M.D., *coach,* University of Wisconsin, University of Missouri, 1918–34; overall coaching record of 290 wins, 101 losses; originator of the laceless basketball and the Meanwell Basketball Shoe

GEORGE L. MIKAN, *college player,* DePaul University, 1944–46; three times all-American, twice College Player of the Year; scored 1,870 points during his college career

HAROLD G. OLSEN, *contributor,* President, N.A.B.C., 1933; responsible for adoption of the ten-second rule; member, Olympic Basketball Committee, 1948

AMOS A. STAGG, *contributor,* a friend of Dr. Naismith, who assisted in the development of the game; played in the first public basketball game, March 11, 1892

JOHN R. WOODEN, *coach,* U.C.L.A., 1948–75; holds the greatest coaching record in college basketball history: eight of nine Pacific Coast titles and N.C.A.A. titles, Coach of the Year, 1964, '67, '69, '70, '72, and '73

ERNEST A. BLOOD, *coach,* Potsdam, New York, high school, 1906–15; *not one* of his Potsdam teams was *ever* defeated

VICTOR A. HANSON, *college player,* Syracuse University, 1925–27; three times all-American, once College Player of the Year

GEORGE T. HEPBRON, *referee,* author of the first book on *How to Play Basketball,* 1904; member, Amateur Athletic Union Rules Committee, 1896–1915; Secretary, Joint Rules Committee, 1915–36

FRANK W. KEANEY, *coach,* University of

Rhode Island, 1920–47; early proponent of fast-break play; coaching record of 401 wins, 124 losses

WARD L. LAMBERT, *coach*, Purdue, 1916–46; pioneer of the fast-break style; coaching record of 371 wins, 152 losses

EDWARD C. MACAULEY, *college player*, St. Louis University, 1946–49; twice all-American, once College Player of the Year; led the nation in field goal percentage with a .524 average in 1946–47

BRANCH McCRACKEN, *college player*, Indiana University, 1928–30; all-American, Western Conference Most Valuable Player, 1928; during his college career he scored 32% of all the Indiana team's points

CHARLES C. MURPHY, *college player*, Purdue, 1928–30; the first of basketball's "big men" at 6 feet 9; twice all-American; set Western Conference and Big Ten scoring record of 143 points in 1929 season

HENRY V. PORTER, *contributor*, organizer of the National Basketball Committee of the U.S. and Canada, 1928; first high school representative on the National Rules Committee; pioneer of the molded basketball, the fan-shaped backboard, and the 29½-inch ball

FORREST S. DE BERNARDI, *A.A.U. player*, A.A.U. all-American, 1921–23

GEORGE H. HOYT, *referee*, organizer of the first Officials' Board, 1920

GEORGE E. KEOGAN, *coach*, Notre Dame, 1923–43; coaching record of 327 wins, 96 losses, a 77% victory average

ROBERT A. KURLAND, *college player*, University of Oklahoma, 1944–46; N.C.A.A. Most Valuable Player, 1946; national scoring leader, 1946

ERNEST C. QUIGLEY, *referee*, officiated in over 1,500 games, 1913–44

JOHN S. ROOSMA, *college player*, West Point, 1924–26; scored 44% of Army's points in one season; totaled 1,100 points in college play

LEONARD D. SACHS, *coach*, Loyola of Chicago, 1924–42; coached his teams to 32 straight wins, 1927–29, and 20 straight wins, 1938–39

ARTHUR A. SCHABINGER, *contributor*, co-founder, N.A.B.C., 1927; director, Olympic Basketball Tournament, 1936

CHRISTIAN STEINMETZ, *college player*, organizer of the first basketball team at the University of Wisconsin, 1905; established records that lasted until 1954: most points in a game (50), most points in a season (462); the first college player ever to score over 1,000 points in college play

DAVID TOBEY, *referee*, professional and collegiate official, 1918–46; author of the first book on basketball officiating, 1944

ARTHUR L. TRESTER, *contributor*, Commissioner, Indiana High School Athletic Association, 1922; established the model upon which nearly all high school tournaments are based

EDWARD A. WACHTER, *pro player*, played on many pro teams from 1896 to 1924; the first professional player to be "sold" to another team, 1902

DAVID H. WALSH, *referee*, Director, Collegiate Officials' Bureau, 1941–56; Secretary-Treasurer, International Association of Approved Basketball Officials, 1948–56

BERNHARD BORGMANN, *pro player*, member, Original Celtics and other early teams, 1921–42; played in 2,500 professional games

JOHN J. O'BRIEN, *contributor*, organizer, Interstate Pro League, 1914; organizer, Metropolitan Basketball League, 1921; President, American Basketball League, 1928–53

ANDY PHILLIP, *college player*, University of Illinois, 1941–43; twice all-American; set Western Conference records for most points (255), most field goals (16), and most points in a game (40) in 1943

JACK McCRACKEN, *A.A.U. player*, A.A.U. all-American seven times between 1932 and 1942

FRANK MORGENWECK, *contributor*, manager, financier, and promoter, 1901–33

HARLAN O. PAGE, *college player*, University of Chicago, 1907–10; this left-handed shooter led his teams to Western Conference Titles in 1907, '09, and '10

BARNEY SEDRAN, *pro player*, played with several different teams from 1912 to 1926; in 1926 he made 17 consecutive field goals from farther than 25 feet from the basket with *no backboard*

LYNN W. ST. JOHN, *contributor*, member, N.C.A.A. Rules Committee for 25 years; Chairman, National Basketball Committee of the U.S. and Canada, 1933–37

JOHN A. THOMPSON, *college player*, Montana State, 1927–30; all-Conference all four years, College Player of the Year, 1929; scored 1,539 points in three years of college play

ROBERT F. GRUENIG, *A.A.U. player*, A.A.U. all-American ten times between 1933 and 1948

WILLIAM A. REID, *contributor*, Vice President, N.C.A.A., 1942–46

JOHN W. BUNN, *contributor*, editor, *Basketball Guide*, 1959–67

HAROLD E. ("BUD") FOSTER, *college player*, University of Wisconsin, 1928–30; once all-American; teams on which he played lost only seven games in three years

NAT HOLMAN, *pro player*, member, Original Celtics, 1921–28; Celtics won 720 out of 795 games during this period

EDWARD S. IRISH, *contributor,* Basketball Director, Madison Square Garden, 1934; founder, New York Knickerbockers, 1946

R. WILLIAM JONES, *contributor,* co-founder, International Amateur Basketball Federation, 1932; organization responsible for spread of basketball to 130 nations; Secretary-General, United Nations International Council of Sport and Physical Education, 1958

KENNETH D. LOEFFLER, *coach,* 1929–57; Geneva College, Yale, LaSalle College, Texas A&M, the St. Louis Bombers; college record of 310 wins; St. Louis Bombers won the 1948 N.B.A. division title

JOHN D. RUSSELL, *pro player,* played more than 3,200 professional games in 28 years with the Brooklyn Visitations, Cleveland Rosenblums, Chicago Bruins, and Rochester Centrals

WALTER A. BROWN, *contributor,* founder, National Basketball Association, 1946; founder, Boston Celtics

PAUL D. HINKLE, *contributor,* Dean of Indiana Coaches; Athletic Director, Butler University, 1927–70; Butler had over 500 wins in 39 seasons and a national title in 1929

HOWARD A. HOBSON, *coach,* Southern Oregon University, University of Oregon, Yale, 1928–56; his 1939 Oregon team won the first N.C.A.A. tournament

WILLIAM G. MOKRAY, *contributor,* publicist, Rhode Island Rams, Boston Celtics, 1929–42; founder, *N.B.A. Guide,* 1959; author, *Ronald Encyclopedia of Basketball,* 1963

EVERETT S. DEAN, *coach,* Carleton College, Indiana University, Stanford, 1921–55; led Carleton to 48 victories in 52 games, 1921–24; led Stanford to N.C.A.A. title in 1942

JOE LAPCHICK, *pro player,* Original Celtics, 1923–29; Cleveland Rosenblums, 1929–31; reorganized Original Celtics, 1930–36

CLAIR F. BEE, *contributor,* coach, Rider College, Long Island University, Baltimore Bullets, New York Military Academy, for 29 years; originator, three-second rule; assisted in the development of the 24-second rule

HOWARD G. CANN, *coach,* New York University, 1922–58; coaching record of 409 wins, 232 losses

AMORY T. GILL, *coach,* Oregon State, 1929–64; led his teams to 599 victories

ALVIN F. JULIAN, *coach,* Albright, Muhlenberg, Holy Cross, Dartmouth, Boston Celtics; led Dartmouth to three Ivy League titles, 1956, '58, '59

ARNOLD J. ("RED") AUERBACH, *coach,* Boston Celtics, 1950–66; led the Celtics to eight consecutive N.B.A. Championships, 1959–66; holds professional coaching record of 1,037 wins, 548 losses; Coach of the Year, 1965

HENRY G. DEHNERT, *player,* Original Celtics, Cleveland Rosenblums, New York Celtics; played for winning team in 1,900 professional games, 1920–39

HENRY P. IBA, *coach,* Oklahoma State University, 1934–70; led his teams to 800 victories; twice U.S. Olympic Team coach, 1964, '68

ADOLPH F. RUPP, *coach,* University of Kentucky, 1930–72; coaching record of 874 wins, 190 losses is the nation's best college coaching average

CHARLES H. TAYLOR, *contributor,* originator, basketball clinic, North Carolina State University, 1922; originator, *Converse Yearbook of Basketball,* 1922; designer, Taylor Basketball Shoe, 1931

BERNARD L. CARNEVALE, *coach,* Cranford High School, U.S. Naval Academy, 1944–66; his high school team accumulated 51 wins in two years; at the Naval Academy, his teams had 257 wins in twenty years

ROBERT E. DAVIES, *player,* Seton Hall College, 1938–41; twice all-American, three times Most Valuable Player; Most Valuable Player, 1942 College All-Star Game; with the Rochester Royals, was the N.B.A.'s leading assist man every year from 1949 to 1955; totaled 7,771 points as a pro; originator of the behind-the-back dribble

ROBERT J. COUSY, *player,* Holy Cross, 1948–50; twice all-American, twice Most Valuable Player; Boston Celtics, 1950–63; professional total of 16,960 points, 6,959 assists; starred in five consecutive N.B.A. title seasons with Boston; dubbed "Mr. Basketball"

ROBERT L. PETTIT, *player,* Louisiana State University, 1952–54; twice all-American, three times Most Valuable Player; N.B.A. Rookie of the Year, 1955; St. Louis Hawks 1955–65; at his retirement in 1965, he was the highest scorer in N.B.A. history with 20,880 points

ABRAHAM M. SAPERSTEIN, *contributor,* founder, player, coach, and manager, the Harlem Globetrotters, 1927–66; the Globetrotters have played to fifty-five million spectators in 87 countries; World Pro Champions, 1940; International Cup Champions, 1943–44

EDGAR A. DIBBLE, *coach,* Western Kentucky University, 1922–64; his teams won or shared in 32 conference titles and participated in three N.C.A.A. and eight N.I.T. tournaments; first college coach to win 1,000 games at a single college

ROBERT L. DOUGLAS, *contributor,* organizer and coach, New York Renaissance ("Rens"), 1922–44; the Rens won 88 consecutive games in 1933, 128 consecutive games in 1934; won a total of 2,318 games in 22 years; no other coach at any level has ever won as many games

PAUL ENDACOTT, *player*, University of Kansas, 1920–23; three times all-conference, he led the Kansas team through an undefeated season to the 1923 national title

MAX FRIEDMAN, *player*, New York Roosevelts; Hudson River League, New York State League, Pennsylvania League; Cleveland Rosenblums, 1909–27

EDWARD GOTTLIEB, *contributor*, organizer, South Philadelphia Hebrew Association team (Sphas), 1918; organizer, owner, manager, Philadelphia Warriors, 1946

W.R. CLIFFORD WELLS, *contributor*, Indiana high school coach, Tulane University coach, for 47 years; founder, Indiana High School Coaches Association, 1935

JOHN BECKMAN, *player*, played with several professional teams, including the New York St. Gabriels and the Original Celtics, 1910–36; team captain of the Celtics, 1922

BRUCE DRAKE, *coach*, University of Oklahoma, 1939–45; coaching record of 200 wins and 6 regional titles; assistant coach, U.S. Olympic team, 1956

ARTHUR C. LONBORG, *coach*, McPherson College, Washburn University, Northwestern University, 1922–50; led his teams to 323 wins

ELMER H. RIPLEY, *contributor*, coach, Harlem Globetrotters, 1953–56; coach, Israel Olympic team, 1956; coach, Canadian Olympic team, 1960

ADOLPH SCHAYES, *player*, New York University all-American, 1948; Syracuse Nationals, 1949–64; player-coach, Philadelphia Seventy-Sixers, led them to the 1966 N.B.A. championship

HARRY A. FISHER, *contributor*, member, original Collegiate Rules Committee, 1905; first full-time coach, Columbia University, 1906–16; coaching record of 101 wins, 39 losses

MAURICE PODOLOFF, *contributor*, President, Basketball Association of America, 1946–49; President, N.B.A., 1949–63; responsible for professional basketball's first television contract in 1954

ERNEST J. SCHMIDT, *player*, Kansas State College, 1930–33; led his team to 47 straight wins and 4 conference titles; led the conference in scoring for three years, 1931–33; all-American, 1932

GREAT MOMENTS IN BASKETBALL

The 24-second clock in professional basketball came about largely as a result of one game— one of the strangest in history. In the late 1940's, professional basketball was being dominated by the great Minneapolis Lakers (eventually to become the Los Angeles Lakers) and their center, George Mikan. Mikan and the

Lakers were such scoring threats that other teams figured the only way to beat them was to keep the ball from them. Still, even teams that stalled seldom won, since the Lakers would gradually edge ahead, and then the pressure would be on the stalling team to shoot more often. Every shot they missed gave the ball to Mikan, who was a tremendous rebounder.

In 1950, the Fort Wayne Pistons (now the Detroit Pistons) arrived in Minneapolis to do battle with the Lakers. The Pistons were good ball handlers, and they knew that the Lakers were not particularly good at stealing the ball —they didn't have to be. So the Pistons agreed on an unusual strategy: They would do everything they could to keep the ball . . . even if it meant not taking many shots.

The Pistons stalled from the opening jump. They dribbled and passed and then dribbled and passed some more. Each player took a turn dribbling the ball around before passing to a teammate.

At the end of the first quarter, the score was Fort Wayne 8, Minneapolis 7. After a boring first half, the score stood at 13–11, in favor of the Lakers. Fans were restless and stirring about; a few had already gone home because of the lack of action.

Those who stayed expected the action to pick up during the third quarter. But they were disappointed. The teams prepared for the final quarter with 17 points for the Lakers and 16 for the Pistons.

Though the game was slow and uninteresting, at least the strategy was working: The Pistons were keeping the score almost even. However, the fans were angrily booing *both* teams.

The fourth quarter? More of the same. Both teams scored a total of only four points in the entire period. With ten seconds left, the Lakers were ahead 18–17, and Fort Wayne had the ball. Larry Faust shot, and the ball sailed over the outstretched hand of George Mikan and through the basket. Fort Wayne won the game 19–18, but there wasn't any cheering.

Maurice Podoloff, president of the N.B.A., realized that professional basketball would die from lack of interest if this type of stalling were to continue. He started at once to look for ways of preventing it. Soon thereafter, experiments began which led to the 24-second rule.

"THE COOZ"

One of the most famous players in the game's history got his start when his name was drawn out of a hat. He had had a fine high school and college basketball career, but he was smaller than most pro players and considered a bit too "flashy" for the pros.

He signed with Tri-Cities, an N.B.A. franchise. But before he could play a game, another team went broke, and a player shuffle resulted, putting him once again up for grabs.

He and two other players were to be "divided" among Boston, New York, and Philadelphia. But there was a problem: All three teams wanted Max Zaslofsky, one of the three, considered to be among the game's best shooters. The league president couldn't decide how to apportion the three players, since all three team owners wanted the same man. Finally it was agreed that the team owners would draw names from a hat. The names of the three players were written on slips of paper, which were dropped into a hat, and the three owners each drew one.

Ned Irish of the New York Knickerbockers drew first and got Zaslofsky. Philadelphia got ball handler Andy Phillip. Walter Brown, own-

er of the Boston Celtics, got the other player. He was disappointed.

But the player himself was elated—the Celtics were the team he had dreamed of playing for. He vowed to earn a spot on the team, since the owner felt he had been "stuck" with him.

Earn a spot he certainly did. His name was Bob Cousy—"The Cooz"—one of the greatest players in the history of the Celtics team and basketball itself.

He led the N.B.A. in assists for eight consecutive years. He played on the all-star team every single year and was voted most valuable player in 1956. Bob Cousy played 917 games in thirteen seasons for the Celtics, making 6,949 assists and 16,955 points. He turned the Celtics into consistent winners, leading them to seven consecutive N.B.A. division championships and five consecutive world championships.

Management changed its opinion of Cooz, of course. When any other coach would boast that a new player was "as good as Cousy," the Celtics personnel would chuckle. Coach Red Auerbach, who hadn't even wanted Cousy at first, would shake his head and say, "There's *nobody* as good as Cousy, and there never *was*."

"THE STILT"

On a cold, snowy February evening in 1949, "Jumpin' Joe" Fulks of the Philadelphia Warriors sank an incredible 63 points during a game with the Jets of Indianapolis. This was in a day when it was considered good if an entire team scored that many points.

Fulks's record stood for ten long years in pro basketball. Then, along came another Philadelphia Warrior, known as "The Stilt" because he was over seven feet tall. His name: Wilt Chamberlain, the single greatest player in basketball.

During the 1961–62 season, Wilt scored 50 points or more in 46 of the team's regular season games, finishing the year with an average 50.4 points per game.

In December, 1961, Chamberlain broke the league scoring record with 78 points (in triple-overtime) during a game against the Lakers. Only a month later, he scored 71 points in a regulation-length game against Chicago. He was a scoring phenomenon with his dunk shots, his one-handed "dippers," and his jump shots. The only shots he wasn't very good at were free throws.

Then came the night of March 2, 1962. The Warriors had second place sewed up and were awaiting the play-offs. Their opponents, the New York Knicks, were in last place. The game was being played on neutral ground, at Hershey, Pennsylvania. The unimportant status of the game was no doubt responsible for the "looseness" of the players, especially Wilt.

The moment the game started, Wilt began to score. More interesting, though, was the fact that he hit ten straight foul shots. He would stand at the line, grin, and toss the ball through with rare precision. Soon the fans began to suspect that something unusual was happening.

At the end of the first quarter, the score was Philadelphia 42, Knicks 26. Wilt had 23 points. In the second quarter, the Knicks tried doubleteaming Wilt, then *triple*-teaming him, but he was playing an inspired game. His personal point total continued to climb as he stuffed shot after shot through the basket. The Warriors led at the half, 79–68, and Wilt's total had climbed to 41 points.

The crowd was excited, sensing a new record in the making. And in the third quarter, Wilt was hotter than ever. He picked up 28 more points, for a total of 69—only 9 points less than his own league-leading record.

With a full quarter left to play, the crowd was ready to witness a new record. They began to chant: "Give it to Wilt! Give it to Wilt!"

The Warriors tried to feed the ball to their big center, and the Knicks tried desperately to stop him from shooting. In only minutes, though, Wilt slammed through his 75th point, but the game was far from over. Soon came Wilt's 76th and 77th points, then 78th and 79th, and a new record was set. The fans thundered their approval.

With five minutes left to play, Wilt had 89

points. The fans were frenzied, anticipating the possibility of a 100-point game for Wilt.

The Knicks certainly didn't want to go down in pro basketball history as the only team to have an individual player score 100 points against them. They decided to abandon individual guarding assignments and concentrate on Chamberlain.

However, no defense can stop foul shots, and Wilt was still hitting them, to the amazement of fans and teammates. The Knicks stalled for as long as the 24-second clock would allow, trying to run out the game before Wilt made his "century." They collapsed their entire defense around him. This strategy only drew more fouls, though, and with three shots from the foul line and a beautiful jump shot, Wilt reached 94 points. The crowd was screaming.

Again the ball came to Wilt. He leaped, twisting, with two Knicks hanging on his great shoulders, and shot the ball. In it went—96 points. Then Wilt stole the ball, leaped, and fired—98 points. There was little more than one minute left to play.

Wilt missed a shot, then missed another. With 46 seconds left to play, he broke under the basket, and a perfect pass hit his hands. Wilt jumped and stuffed the ball through the basket.

The final 46 seconds of that game were never played. Even though the clock continued to run, fans and players from both sides streamed onto the court to congratulate the big man. The buzzer sounded amid the pandemonium, ending the game at 169–147.

The great Wilt Chamberlain had made 36 field goals and 28 of 32 foul shots for a total of 100 points. This record may never be equaled in professional basketball. No other player has even come close.

CHAPTER 10

BASKETBALL TERMS

All-American—the outstanding players in college basketball, selected annually by sportswriters and college coaches

All-Court Press—defensive alignment in which defenders cover offensive players closely, regardless of their position on the floor

All-Pro—the outstanding players in professional basketball, selected annually by sportswriters and coaches

Assist—a pass to an open player that results directly in a field goal

Backboard—the rectangular or fan-shaped surface to which the basket is attached

Backcourt—that half of the playing court, from end line to center line, *opposite* the half in which the offensive action is taking place; changes each time possession of the ball changes between teams

Bank Shot—a shot in which the ball is bounced off the backboard

Baseball Pass—a long, one-handed pass, often used to begin a fast break

Baseline—*see* End Line

Basket—the metal ring, 18 inches in diameter, with a funnel-shaped net attached, through which the ball must pass for a field goal

Blocking—any physical contact by a player that impedes the progress of an opponent

Boards—the backboards

Bonus Shot—an extra attempt to make a free throw, awarded to a player after the fouling team has committed more than four personal fouls in any quarter

Bounce Pass—a pass in which the ball is caromed (bounced once) off the floor to a receiver instead of thrown directly to him

Bucket—slang for field goal

Buzzer—the signal used to end each period of play; also called the horn

Center—team position usually held by the tallest man on a team, whose area of responsibility is generally closest to the basket

Center Circle—a circle 12 feet in diameter, in the center of the playing floor, from which each period of play begins with a jump ball

Center Line—the 2-inch-wide line dividing the court in half at its width; also called the ten-second line, since the offensive team must take the ball across it within ten seconds of gaining possession

Charging—physical contact with a defender by an offensive player in possession of the ball; an offensive foul

Charity Stripe—slang for free throw line

Clearing the Boards—the act of gaining possession of a rebound and successfully initiating a new offensive play

Collapsing Defense—defensive alignment in which defensive players crowd around one offensive player, usually the center

Cut—a quick change of direction by a player

Disqualification—the removal of a player from the game after he has committed six personal fouls (five in high school and college)

Double Dribble—the act of dribbling with both

hands at once, or dribbling, stopping the dribble, then dribbling again

Double Foul—two fouls occurring at once, committed by both teams; no free throws are awarded; play is resumed with a jump ball

Double-Team—to guard one offensive player with two defenders

Dribble—a method of moving the ball from place to place by bouncing it continuously as the player in possession moves

Drive—an offensive play in which the player, with or without possession of the ball, moves quickly and directly toward the basket

Dunk—a shot or attempted shot in which the ball is pushed directly through the basket with one or both hands; also called a stuff or jam; at present, legal only in professional play

End Line—the boundary line at either end of the court behind the basket

Fast Break—an offensive strategy in which the ball is moved into position for a shot as quickly as possible after possession is gained, before the defense has time to react

Feed—the act of passing or handing the ball to a teammate

Field Goal—a 2-point score

Forward—team position held by two players whose areas of responsibility are generally on either side of the free throw lane and basket

Foul—any infraction of the rules resulting in either a free throw or loss of possession and counting toward individual player's disqualification from the game

Foul Circle—a circle 12 feet in diameter, the diameter of which rests on the foul line

Foul Lane—an area 19 feet long and 16 feet wide (12 feet wide in college and high school) that extends from the end line to the free throw line; no offensive player can remain in this area for longer than three seconds, with or without the ball

Foul Line—the line at the end of the foul lane, 16 feet long, behind which free throw attempts must be made; it is 13 feet 9 inches from the foul line to the center of the basket

Foul Out—to be disqualified

Free Throw—an unobstructed attempt to make a shot from the foul line, awarded to a player who has been fouled; a successful free throw counts 1 point

Front Court—that half of the playing court, from end line to center line, in which the offensive action is taking place; changes each time possession of the ball changes between teams

Full-Court Press—*see* All-Court Press

Goal—a successful field goal

Guard—team position held by two players whose general areas of responsibility are farthest from the basket on either side of the court

Held Ball—a situation in which possession is disputed between two opposing players; will be resolved by a jump ball between those players

High Post—a position on the floor occupied by the center, beyond the end of the foul lane (*see also* Low Post)

Holding—the act of grasping an opponent by his body or uniform to impede his progress; a personal foul

Intentional Foul—a foul committed on purpose, usually to stop the clock and attempt to gain possession with a rebound after a free throw

Interception—the catching of a pass intended for one player by a player of the opposing team

Jump Ball—a method of beginning each period of play and settling disputed possession; the ball is thrown straight up by an official, and one member of each team attempts to control it

Keyhole—the area beneath the basket, indicated by the foul lane and the foul circle

Loose Ball—the ball in play, with neither team having possession

Loose Ball Foul—a foul committed when neither team has possession of the ball

Low Post—a position on the floor occupied by the center, close to the basket on either side of the foul lane

Man-to-Man—a defensive alignment in which each individual player guards one individual offensive player; also called one-on-one

Overtime—an extra period, or periods, of play after a game has ended in a tie during regulation time

Period—one complete segment of playing time

Pick—an offensive maneuver in which a player passes close by a stationary teammate, in an attempt to break away from the defensive player following him

Pivot Man—the center, around whom offensive action usually revolves

Playmaker—a player on the team who uses hand or verbal signals to call for specific formations or patterns by his teammates; an excellent passer who initiates a play sequence

Rebound—to control or gain possession of a ball that has bounced away from the basket or backboard after an unsuccessful shot

Referee—an official responsible for starting the play with a jump ball or by handing the ball to a player; also responsible for stopping the play whenever a foul is committed or the rules are violated

Sagging Defense—*see* Collapsing Defense

Scorer—an official responsible for recording all game statistics, including number of points made by individual players and number of fouls committed

Screen—an offensive maneuver in which a player positions himself between a teammate in possession of the ball and the defensive player who is guarding that teammate

Set Offense—any offensive maneuver that follows a prearranged pattern or sequence

Shot—any attempt to score a field goal by projecting the ball through the basket; types of shots include the set shot, jump shot, hook shot, lay-up, and tip-in

Sidelines—the side boundaries of the playing area

Strong Side—that half of an offensive formation, on either side of the basket, that includes the center

Substitute—a player from the bench who takes the place of a teammate who has been injured or disqualified

Swish—slang for a "perfect" field goal, when the ball goes through the basket without touching the rim or backboard

Throw In—to put the ball in play with a pass from out-of-bounds

Timer—an official responsible for stopping the play at the end of each designated period by sounding a buzzer or horn; also responsible for stopping the game clock each time a foul is committed or time-out is called

Traveling—illegal movement by a player in possession of the ball, who cannot take more than one step in any direction without dribbling

Turnover—a loss of ball possession by a team that has failed to score

Umpire—another title for Referee

Violation—an infraction of the rules resulting in loss of ball possession

Walking—*see* Traveling